THE TIMES OF MY LIFE
a journal of personal discovery

The Times of My Life

By Jeanne Taylor McClellan
With Debbi Hines

Published by
jmcclellanpublishing
West Grove, PA

Copyright 2018 by Jeanne Taylor McClellan

For information and ordering contact: jmcclellanpublishing
www.jeannetaylormcclellan.com

All rights reserved. No part of this book may be reproduced or transmitted in any manner-graphic, electronic or mechanical, including photocopying, recording or by any information storage and retrieval system whatsoever without the written permission of the author except in the case of brief quotations embodied in critical articles and reviews.

ISBN 978-0-692-19946-6

Printed in the United States of America

THE TIMES OF MY LIFE
a journal of personal discovery

Jeanne Taylor McClellan
with
Debbi Hines

jmcclellanpublishing 2018

Also by Jeanne Taylor McClellan
Stars in the Sea: stories of hope, happiness, and helping hands

With Debbi Hines:
The FUNctional Facilitator: Because attitude is everything!

About the Authors

Jeanne McClellan is a personal development coach and management consultant with extensive experience in organizational effectiveness, people development, and team building. She holds degrees in education and adult counseling. She is the CEO of J. Taylor Consulting, a management-consulting firm. In her coaching work, Jeanne has realized the value that memories bring to the growth and development of individuals. She and her husband live in Chester County, PA.

Debbi Hines has a professional background in training, customer service, and program development in healthcare, relocation, and tutoring programs. She has a deep passion and love for family and believes family history provides much insight into our current lives. Debbi lives with her husband and energetic, funny 3 year-old son.

We dedicate this journal
to our families and friends, here and gone,
who are always part of
The Times of Our Lives.

With thanks...

To our families, friends, co-workers, and acquaintances who have helped us to create The Times of Our Lives, especially...

...my Mema, Nonnon, Uncle George, and Aunt Tess who filled my life with music, laughter, and wonderful food; and four special friends who play a major part in my life still today ~ *Jeanne*

... my loving parents and sister, grandparents, and aunts/uncles who directly and indirectly emphasized the importance of family and its history. You all helped to create an idyllic childhood that I can only hope to pass on to my son. ~ *Debbi*

Table of Contents

The Value of Journaling   2

Examples From The Authors   3

Directions   4

My First 5 Years   6

My Childhood Years   10

My Teenager Years   14

My Twenties   18

My Thirties   22

My Forties   26

My Fifties   30

My Sixties   34

My Seventies   38

My Eighties   42

My Nineties   46

More Thoughts   50

Thoughts From The Authors   54

The Value of Journaling

Journaling is a beneficial tool for many reasons- stress reduction, decision-making, processing challenging times, etc. and Times of My Life can add the following benefits as well:

Activity for Memory Loss. Memory loss is often devastating for the whole family but those experiencing memory loss can often share gems of information from their life long ago. This workbook is an excellent activity to engage family members in a positive way and record their memories for posterity. Those with memory loss may also enjoy reading and rereading the entries.
- *Before my Gram experienced later stages of dementia, she asked us to write down some of her memories. As her dementia progressed, we would often find her rereading those memories over and over. You could tell she enjoyed them!*

Activity for Caregivers. Dealing with memory loss or aging is a draining experience. By using Times of Your Life, you can explore the happy memories by yourself or with your loved one to develop a deeper bond and have a greater appreciation for the life that your family experienced.
- *My mother was the caregiver for her mom. She found the best conversations with her mom were about her mom's childhood. Those conversations allowed for my mother to understand her mom better and also have engaging visits.*

Leave a Legacy. This workbook can be a record of your early life for future generations. Share the joys and sorrows that they might not know. Learning about your past allows them to understand you better.
- *I wanted my children to know that things didn't come easily to me, as it might have looked on the outside. Sharing the ups and downs of life allowed them to see my journey.*

Celebrate successes of the past. We often forget all of our positive achievements in our life, but journaling can offer a written record of these successes. When people actually see the list of accomplishments and successes of their life written down, it can be very powerful to you and your family and friends.
- *Did I really accomplish all those things in my 20's??*

Accountability for challenges. We learn a lot from mistakes and challenges in our life. By writing them down, we can realize how far we have come from those specific challenges and see the outcome of our choices. While mistakes and challenges are difficult at the time, the lessons we learn from them can impact our entire lives.
- *That job I had in my 30's didn't work out so well for us, but looking back, I see now that it helped me find my dream job in my 40's and beyond.*

Examples From The Authors

Here's a time in Jeanne's life ….

Music: Music has always been a major part of my life. I can thank my Aunt Tess for that. So when I began writing my story my Aunt Tess was an instant entry. My mind began to fill with some wonderful sights and sounds.

From ages 5 – 12, I heard Enrico Caruso and Mario Lanza pouring from her 45rpm record player. Now I can close my eyes and see her singing opera into the curved handle of the vacuum cleaner as she dances around the living room with the windows wide open so that all of the neighbors (and the people walking by our house) could share in her joy of that music. My mind fast forwards and I am 25 years old. I see her holding my baby daughters in her arms and dancing them around the living room singing along with Julius LaRosa and Perry Como. That memory puts a smile on my face that carries me through the rest of my day.

And here's a time from Debbi's life…

Activities: During my childhood, I remember my parents reading to me. Today I can picture my mom reading Mary Poppins to me as we sit together on the front steps waiting for the school bus. I can see the pond out our front door and at the same time I also have visions of all that she's reading to me. At bedtime I hear my dad's rumbling voice as I lay my head on his chest. I smell his faint aftershave and feel his stubble when he kisses me good night. During both of these reading sessions the voices of my parents wrap around me like a cocoon making me feel safe, secure and beyond content. Now when I hear them reading to my own 3 year old son those familiar feelings of contentment wash over me and I can see that my own son feels them too.

Ok, these stories are from the times of our lives. Now it's your turn.

Directions

Step 1:
- Think about your life at each age.

- What are the first memories that pop into your mind? Let the memories enter your mind – see them/hear them/sense them totally. There are no right or wrong memories. They are just the times of your life that have contributed to the person you are today.

Step 2:
- Fill in the corresponding pages but don't worry about spelling or grammar or neatness because this is your story. Feel free to draw pictures or just write and let the journey happen

Step 3:
- Now stop writing and go do something else this is a lot of work for your brain, so let it rest. You can pick up your story any time you want and continue your journey through time.

Step 4:
- Fill in the open-ended questions. As the memories flow you can connect/reconnect with relatives and friends who are part of your journey. Enjoy the experience with them. Always remember though that these are your memories and they are probably a little different from the memories of others who were with you on that journey. We all see things through our own filters and that's what makes us special.

Repeat steps 2 – 4 as many times as you need/want and add pages if you want. Have fun with this. Each memory will bring another memory. Allow yourself to go with the flow.

THE TIMES OF MY LIFE
a journal of personal discovery

written by

(your name)

The dates were: **My First 5 Years**

"There is no friend like someone who has known you since you were five." ~Anne Stevenson

My FAMILY included:

Important/Special PLACES were:

I went to SCHOOL:

My HEALTH was:

I TRAVELED to:

The MUSIC I listened to:

Memorable MEALS/FOODS:

The CHANGES that happened:

My FRIENDS were:

My favorite TOYS were:

ACTIVITIES I enjoyed were:

Thoughts From My First Five Years

Thoughts From My First Five Years

The dates were: My Childhood, 6-12yrs

> *"I love those random memories that make me smile*
> *no matter what is going on in my life right now."* ~www.imfunny.net

My FAMILY included:

Important/Special PLACES were:

I went to SCHOOL:

My HEALTH was:

I TRAVELED to:

The MUSIC I listened to:

Memorable MEALS/FOODS:

The CHANGES that happened:

My FRIENDS were:

My favorite TOYS were:

ACTIVITIES I enjoyed were:

Thoughts From My Childhood

Thoughts From My Childhood

The dates were: **My Teen Years, 12-19yrs**

"Good times become good memories, bad times become good lessons." ~Krexy.com

My FAMILY included:

Important/Special PLACES were:

I went to SCHOOL:

I WORKED at:

My HEALTH was:

I TRAVELED to:

The MUSIC I listened to:

Memorable MEALS/FOODS:

The CHANGES that happened:

My FRIENDS were:

My favorite THINGS were:

ACTIVITIES I enjoyed were:

Thoughts From My Teen Years

Thoughts From My Teen Years

The dates were: **My Twenties**

"Perhaps this is the moment for which you were created." ~Esther 4:14

My FAMILY included:

Important/Special PLACES were:

I went to SCHOOL:

I WORKED at:

My HEALTH was:

I TRAVELED to:

The MUSIC I listened to:

Memorable MEALS/FOODS:

The CHANGES that happened:

My FRIENDS were:

My favorite THINGS were:

ACTIVITIES I enjoyed were:

Thoughts From My Twenties

Thoughts From My Twenties

The dates were: **My Thirties**

"It takes courage to grow up and become who we really are." ~ee cummings

My FAMILY included:

Important/Special PLACES were:

I WORKED at:

My HEALTH was:

I TRAVELED to:

The MUSIC I listened to:

Memorable MEALS/FOODS:

The CHANGES that happened:

My FRIENDS were:

My favorite THINGS were:

ACTIVITIES I enjoyed were:

Thoughts From My Thirties

Thoughts From My Thirties

The dates were: **My Forties**

> *"You see, it's never the environment, it's never the events in our lives, but the meaning we attach to the event – how we interpret them – that shapes who we are today and who we'll become tomorrow."* ~Tony Robbins

My FAMILY included:

Important/Special PLACES were:

I WORKED at:

My HEALTH was:

I TRAVELED to:

The MUSIC I listened to:

Memorable MEALS/FOODS:

The CHANGES that happened:

My FRIENDS were:

My favorite THINGS were:

ACTIVITIES I enjoyed were:

Thoughts From My Forties

Thoughts From My Forties

The dates were: **My Fifties**

> *"To me…old age is always 15 years older than I am…"* ~Bernard Baruch

My FAMILY included:

Important/Special PLACES were:

I WORKED at:

My HEALTH was:

I TRAVELED to:

The MUSIC I listened to:

Memorable MEALS/FOODS:

The CHANGES that happened:

My FRIENDS were:

My favorite THINGS were:

ACTIVITIES I enjoyed were:

Thoughts From My Fifties

Thoughts From My Fifties

The dates were: **My Sixties**

> *Time is not free, but it is priceless.*
> *You can't own it, but you can use it.*
> *You can't keep it but you can spend it.*
> *Once you've lost it you can never get it back.*
> *~Harvey Mackay*

My FAMILY included:

Important/Special PLACES were:

I WORKED at:

My HEALTH was:

I TRAVELED to:

The MUSIC I listened to:

Memorable MEALS/FOODS:

The CHANGES that happened:

My FRIENDS were:

My favorite THINGS were:

ACTIVITIES I enjoyed were:

Thoughts From My Sixties

Thoughts From My Sixties

The dates were: **My Seventies**

"Where did the years go?"

My FAMILY included:

Important/Special PLACES were:

I WORKED at:

My HEALTH was:

I TRAVELED to:

The MUSIC I listened to:

Memorable MEALS/FOODS:

The CHANGES that happened:

My FRIENDS were:

My favorite THINGS were:

ACTIVITIES I enjoyed were:

Thoughts From My Seventies

Thoughts From My Seventies

The dates were: **My Eighties**

> *The trouble is, you think you have the time. ~Buddha*

My FAMILY included:

Important/Special PLACES were:

I WORKED at:

My HEALTH was:

I TRAVELED to:

The MUSIC I listened to:

Memorable MEALS/FOODS:

The CHANGES that happened:

My FRIENDS were:

My favorite THINGS were:

ACTIVITIES I enjoyed were:

Thoughts From My Eighties

Thoughts From My Eighties

The dates were: **My Nineties**

> *"The greatest gift you can give someone is your time because when you give your time, you are giving a portion of your life that you will never get back."* ~Anonymous

My FAMILY included:

Important/Special PLACES were:

I WORKED at:

My HEALTH was:

I TRAVELED to:

The MUSIC I listened to:

Memorable MEALS/FOODS:

The CHANGES that happened:

My FRIENDS were:

My favorite THINGS were:

ACTIVITIES I enjoyed were:

Thoughts From My Nineties

Thoughts From My Nineties

Thoughts From My Life

I am proud that I...

Thoughts From My Life

If I could do it over again...

Thoughts From My Life

What I would tell my younger self...

Thoughts From My Life

I would tell others...

Thoughts From the Authors:

You've put some time and effort into sharing the times of your life and now the next steps are up to you. Here are some things Jeanne and Debbi decided to do with their memories:

- Share memories with family, especially children and grandchildren.

- Include photos from your life to enhance your memories.

- Connect/reconnect with the special people who were impactful.

- Visit/revisit places that came up in your memories.

We would love to hear how you are using this workbook. You can reach us by email at timesofmylife@yahoo.com. We look forward to hearing from you.

Made in the USA
Middletown, DE
16 September 2022